MznLnx

Missing Links Exam Preps

Exam Prep for

Customer Relationship Management : A Databased Approach

Kumar & Reinartz, 1st Edition

The MznLnx Exam Prep is your link from the texbook and lecture to your exams.
The MznLnx Exam Preps are unauthorized and comprehensive reviews of your textbooks.

All material provided by MznLnx and Rico Publications (c) 2010
Textbook publishers and textbook authors do not particpate in or contribute to these reviews.

MznLnx

Rico
Publications

Exam Prep for Customer Relationship Management : A Databased Approach
1st Edition
Kumar & Reinartz

Publisher: Raymond Houge
Assistant Editor: Michael Rouger
Text and Cover Designer: Lisa Buckner
Marketing Manager: Sara Swagger
Project Manager, Editorial Production: Jerry Emerson
Art Director: Vernon Lowerui

Product Manager: Dave Mason
Editorial Assitant: Rachel Guzmanji
Pedagogy: Debra Long
Cover Image: Jim Reed/Getty Images
Text and Cover Printer: City Printing, Inc.
Compositor: Media Mix, Inc.

(c) 2010 Rico Publications
ALL RIGHTS RESERVED. No part of this work covered by the copyright may be reproduced or used in any form or by an means--graphic, electronic, or mechanical, including photocopying, recording, taping, Web distribution, information storage, and retrieval systems, or in any other manner--without the written permission of the publisher.

Printed in the United States
ISBN:

For more information about our products, contact us at:
Dave.Mason@RicoPublications.com

For permission to use material from this text or product, submit a request online to:
Dave.Mason@RicoPublications.com

Contents

CHAPTER 1
CRM, DATABASE MARKETING, AND CUSTOMER VALUE   1

CHAPTER 2
CRM INDUSTRY LANDSCAPE   8

CHAPTER 3
STRATEGIC CRM   12

CHAPTER 4
IMPLEMENTING THE CRM STRATEGY   18

CHAPTER 5
INTRODUCTION TO CUSTOMER-BASED MARKETING METRICS   25

CHAPTER 6
CUSTOMER VALUE METRICS-CONCEPTS AND PRACTICES   29

CHAPTER 7
USING DATABASES   32

CHAPTER 8
DESIGNING LOYALTY PROGRAMS   34

CHAPTER 9
EFFECTIVENESS OF LOYALTY PROGRAMS   38

CHAPTER 10
DATA MINING   41

CHAPTER 11
CAMPAIGN MANAGEMENT   44

CHAPTER 12
APPLICATIONS OF DATABASE MARKETING IN B-TO-C AND B-TO-B SCENARIOS   51

CHAPTER 13
APPLICATION OF THE CUSTOMER VALUE FRAMEWORK TO MARKETING DECISIONS   53

CHAPTER 14
IMPACT OF CRM ON MARKETING CHANNELS   56

ANSWER KEY   63

TO THE STUDENT

COMPREHENSIVE

The *MznLnx* Exam Prep series is designed to help you pass your exams. Editors at MznLnx review your textbooks and then prepare these practice exams to help you master the textbook material. Unlike study guides, workbooks, and practice tests provided by the texbook publisher and textbook authors, *MznLnx* gives you **all** of the material in each chapter in exam form, not just samples, so you can be sure to nail your exam.

MECHANICAL

The MznLnx Exam Prep series creates exams that will help you learn the subject matter as well as test you on your understanding. Each question is designed to help you master the concept. Just working through the exams, you gain an understanding of the subject--its a simple mechanical process that produces success.

INTEGRATED STUDY GUIDE AND REVIEW

MznLnx is not just a set of exams designed to test you, its also a comprehensive review of the subject content. Each exam question is also a review of the concept, making sure that you will get the answer correct without having to go to other sources of material. You learn as you go! Its the easiest way to pass an exam.

HUMOR

Studying can be tedious and dry. MznLnx's instructional design includes moderate humor within the exam questions on occassion, to break the tedium and revitalize the brain

Chapter 1. CRM, DATABASE MARKETING, AND CUSTOMER VALUE

1. _____ was a writer, management consultant, and self-described 'social ecologist.' Widely considered to be the father of 'modern management,' his 39 books and countless scholarly and popular articles explored how humans are organized across all sectors of society--in business, government and the nonprofit world. His writings have predicted many of the major developments of the late twentieth century, including privatization and decentralization; the rise of Japan to economic world power; the decisive importance of marketing; and the emergence of the information society with its necessity of lifelong learning. In 1959, Drucker coined the term 'knowledge worker' and later in his life considered knowledge work productivity to be the next frontier of management.
    a. Peter Ferdinand Drucker
    b. Paschal Eze
    c. Rick Boyce
    d. Nouveau riche

2. _____ is a term commonly used to describe commerce transactions between businesses like the one between a manufacturer and a wholesaler or a wholesaler and a retailer i.e both the buyer and the seller are business entity.This is unlike business-to-consumers (B2C) which involve a business entity and end consumer, or business-to-government (B2G) which involve a business entity and government.

The volume of B2B transactions is much higher than the volume of B2C transactions. The primary reason for this is that in a typical supply chain there will be many B2B transactions involving subcomponent or raw materials, and only one B2C transaction, specifically sale of the finished product to the end customer.

    a. Customer relationship management
    b. Disruptive technology
    c. Social marketing
    d. Business-to-business

3. _____ consists of the processes a company uses to track and organize its contacts with its current and prospective customers. _____ software is used to support these processes; information about customers and customer interactions can be entered, stored and accessed by employees in different company departments. Typical _____ goals are to improve services provided to customers, and to use customer contact information for targeted marketing.
    a. Demand generation
    b. Product bundling
    c. Commercialization
    d. Customer relationship management

4. A _____ is a structured collection of records or data that is stored in a computer system. The structure is achieved by organizing the data according to a _____ model. The model in most common use today is the relational model.

a. Database
b. Power III
c. 6-3-5 Brainwriting
d. 180SearchAssistant

5. _____ is a form of direct marketing using databases of customers or potential customers to generate personalized communications in order to promote a product or service for marketing purposes. The method of communication can be any addressable medium, as in direct marketing.

The distinction between direct and _____ stems primarily from the attention paid to the analysis of data.

a. Power III
b. Database marketing
c. Direct Marketing Associations
d. Direct marketing

6. _____ is a sub-discipline and type of marketing. There are two main definitional characteristics which distinguish it from other types of marketing. The first is that it attempts to send its messages directly to consumers, without the use of intervening media.

a. Database marketing
b. Direct marketing
c. Direct Marketing Associations
d. Power III

7. _____ is the realization of an application idea, model, design, specification, standard, algorithm an _____ is a realization of a technical specification or algorithm as a program, software component, or other computer system. Many _____s may exist for a given specification or standard.

a. AMAX
b. Implementation
c. ACNielsen
d. ADTECH

8. _____ is defined by the American _____ Association as the activity, set of institutions, and processes for creating, communicating, delivering, and exchanging offerings that have value for customers, clients, partners, and society at large. The term developed from the original meaning which referred literally to going to market, as in shopping, or going to a market to sell goods or services.

_____ practice tends to be seen as a creative industry, which includes advertising, distribution and selling.

Chapter 1. CRM, DATABASE MARKETING, AND CUSTOMER VALUE 3

   a. Customer acquisition management
   b. Product naming
   c. Marketing myopia
   d. Marketing

9. Customer _____ consists of the processes a company uses to track and organize its contacts with its current and prospective customers. CRelationship management software is used to support these processes; information about customers and customer interactions can be entered, stored and accessed by employees in different company departments. Typical CRelationship management goals are to improve services provided to customers, and to use customer contact information for targeted marketing.
   a. Green marketing
   b. Product bundling
   c. Marketing
   d. Relationship management

10. _____ is a broad label that refers to any individuals or households that use goods and services generated within the economy. The concept of a _____ is used in different contexts, so that the usage and significance of the term may vary.

A _____ is a person who uses any product or service.

   a. 6-3-5 Brainwriting
   b. 180SearchAssistant
   c. Power III
   d. Consumer

11. _____ or _____ data refers to selected population characteristics as used in government, marketing or opinion research, or the _____ profiles used in such research. Note the distinction from the term 'demography' Commonly-used _____ include race, age, income, disabilities, mobility (in terms of travel time to work or number of vehicles available), educational attainment, home ownership, employment status, and even location.
   a. AStore
   b. Albert Einstein
   c. Demographic
   d. African Americans

Chapter 1. CRM, DATABASE MARKETING, AND CUSTOMER VALUE

12. The _____ is a model used to represent the process of explaining the transformation of countries from high birth rates and high death rates to low birth rates and low death rates as part of the economic development of a country from a pre-industrial to an industrialized economy. It is based on an interpretation begun in 1929 by the American demographer Warren Thompson of prior observed changes, or transitions, in birth and death rates in industrialized societies over the past two hundred years.

Most developed countries are beyond stage three of the model; the majority of developing countries are in stage 2 or stage 3.

a. 180SearchAssistant
b. Power III
c. 6-3-5 Brainwriting
d. Demographic transition model

13. A _____ is the space, actual or metaphorical, in which a market operates. The term is also used in a trademark law context to denote the actual consumer environment, ie. the 'real world' in which products and services are provided and consumed.
a. Power III
b. Marketplace
c. 6-3-5 Brainwriting
d. 180SearchAssistant

14. A personal and cultural _____ is a relative ethic _____, an assumption upon which implementation can be extrapolated. A _____ system is a set of consistent _____s and measures that is soo not true. A principle _____ is a foundation upon which other _____s and measures of integrity are based.
a. Package-on-Package
b. Supreme Court of the United States
c. Perceptual maps
d. Value

15. _____ refer to a collection of facts usually collected as the result of experience, observation or experiment or a set of premises. This may consist of numbers, words particularly as measurements or observations of a set of variables. _____ are often viewed as a lowest level of abstraction from which information and knowledge are derived.
a. Sample size
b. Pearson product-moment correlation coefficient
c. Mean
d. Data

Chapter 1. CRM, DATABASE MARKETING, AND CUSTOMER VALUE

16. _____ refers to the structured transmission of data between organizations by electronic means. It is used to transfer electronic documents from one computer system to another (ie) from one trading partner to another trading partner. It is more than mere E-mail; for instance, organizations might replace bills of lading and even checks with appropriate _____ messages.
    a. AMAX
    b. ACNielsen
    c. ADTECH
    d. Electronic Data Interchange

17. The term _____ is used to describe countries that have a high level of development according to some criteria. Which criteria, and which countries are classified as being developed, is a contentious issue and there is fierce debate about this. Economic criteria have tended to dominate discussions.
    a. Bringin' Home the Oil
    b. Completely randomized designs
    c. Brando
    d. Developed country

18. In calculus, a function f defined on a subset of the real numbers with real values is called _____, if for all x and y such that x ≤ y one has f(x) ≤ f(y), so f preserves the order. In layman's terms, the sign of the slope is always positive (the curve tending upwards) or zero (i.e., non-decreasing, or asymptotic, or depicted as a horizontal, flat line) Likewise, a function is called monotonically decreasing (non-increasing) if, whenever x ≤ y, then f(x) ≥ f(y), so it reverses the order.
    a. Power III
    b. Monotonic
    c. 6-3-5 Brainwriting
    d. 180SearchAssistant

19. _____ is an advertisement in which a particular product specifically mentions a competitor by name for the express purpose of showing why the competitor is inferior to the product naming it.

This should not be confused with parody advertisements, where a fictional product is being advertised for the purpose of poking fun at the particular advertisement, nor should it be confused with the use of a coined brand name for the purpose of comparing the product without actually naming an actual competitor. ('Wikipedia tastes better and is less filling than the Encyclopedia Galactica.')

In the 1980s, during what has been referred to as the cola wars, soft-drink manufacturer Pepsi ran a series of advertisements where people, caught on hidden camera, in a blind taste test, chose Pepsi over rival Coca-Cola.

a. Cost per conversion
b. GL-70
c. Heavy-up
d. Comparative advertising

20. _____ measures the performance of a system. Certain goals are defined and the _____ gives the percentage to which they should be achieved.

Examples

- Percentage of calls answered in a call center.
- Percentage of customers waiting less than a given fixed time.
- Percentage of customers that do not experience a stock out.

_____ is used in supply chain management and in inventory management to measure the performance of inventory systems.

Under stochastic conditions it is unavoidable that in some periods the inventory on hand is not sufficient to deliver the complete demand and, as a consequence, that part of the demand is filled only after an inventory-related waiting time.

a. False designation of origin
b. Symbol group
c. Nielsen SoundScan
d. Service level

21. _____s are structured marketing efforts that reward, and therefore encourage, loyal buying behaviour -- behaviour which is potentially of benefit to the firm.

In marketing generally and in retailing more specifically, a loyalty card, rewards card, points card, advantage card, or club card is a plastic or paper card, visually similar to a credit card or debit card, that identifies the card holder as a member in a _____. Loyalty cards are a system of the loyalty business model.

a. 180SearchAssistant
b. 6-3-5 Brainwriting
c. Power III
d. Loyalty program

22. Procter is a surname, and may also refer to:

- Bryan Waller Procter (pseud. Barry Cornwall), English poet
- Goodwin Procter, American law firm
- _____, consumer products multinational

a. Black PRies
b. Procter ' Gamble
c. Convergent
d. Flyer

Chapter 2. CRM INDUSTRY LANDSCAPE

1. _____ is the provision of service to customers before, during and after a purchase.

According to Turban et al., '_____ is a series of activities designed to enhance the level of customer satisfaction - that is, the feeling that a product or service has met the customer expectation.'

Its importance varies by product, industry and customer.

   a. COPC Inc.
   b. Facing
   c. Customer service
   d. Customer experience

2. _____ is defined by the American _____ Association as the activity, set of institutions, and processes for creating, communicating, delivering, and exchanging offerings that have value for customers, clients, partners, and society at large. The term developed from the original meaning which referred literally to going to market, as in shopping, or going to a market to sell goods or services.

_____ practice tends to be seen as a creative industry, which includes advertising, distribution and selling.

   a. Product naming
   b. Marketing myopia
   c. Customer acquisition management
   d. Marketing

3. Sales force management systems are information systems used in marketing and management that help automate some sales and sales force management functions. They are frequently combined with a marketing information system, in which case they are often called Customer Relationship Management (CRM) systems.

_____ Systems, typically a part of a company's customer relationship management system, is a system that automatically records all the stages in a sales process.

   a. 180SearchAssistant
   b. Sales force automation
   c. 6-3-5 Brainwriting
   d. Power III

4. _____ is an advertisement in which a particular product specifically mentions a competitor by name for the express purpose of showing why the competitor is inferior to the product naming it.

Chapter 2. CRM INDUSTRY LANDSCAPE

This should not be confused with parody advertisements, where a fictional product is being advertised for the purpose of poking fun at the particular advertisement, nor should it be confused with the use of a coined brand name for the purpose of comparing the product without actually naming an actual competitor. ('Wikipedia tastes better and is less filling than the Encyclopedia Galactica.')

In the 1980s, during what has been referred to as the cola wars, soft-drink manufacturer Pepsi ran a series of advertisements where people, caught on hidden camera, in a blind taste test, chose Pepsi over rival Coca-Cola.

- a. Heavy-up
- b. GL-70
- c. Cost per conversion
- d. Comparative advertising

5. _____ consists of the processes a company uses to track and organize its contacts with its current and prospective customers. _____ software is used to support these processes; information about customers and customer interactions can be entered, stored and accessed by employees in different company departments. Typical _____ goals are to improve services provided to customers, and to use customer contact information for targeted marketing.
- a. Customer relationship management
- b. Product bundling
- c. Commercialization
- d. Demand generation

6. Customer _____ consists of the processes a company uses to track and organize its contacts with its current and prospective customers. CRelationship management software is used to support these processes; information about customers and customer interactions can be entered, stored and accessed by employees in different company departments. Typical CRelationship management goals are to improve services provided to customers, and to use customer contact information for targeted marketing.
- a. Green marketing
- b. Relationship management
- c. Marketing
- d. Product bundling

7. _____s are structured marketing efforts that reward, and therefore encourage, loyal buying behaviour -- behaviour which is potentially of benefit to the firm.

In marketing generally and in retailing more specifically, a loyalty card, rewards card, points card, advantage card, or club card is a plastic or paper card, visually similar to a credit card or debit card, that identifies the card holder as a member in a _____. Loyalty cards are a system of the loyalty business model.

a. 6-3-5 Brainwriting
b. 180SearchAssistant
c. Loyalty program
d. Power III

8. In finance, an _____ is a contract between a buyer and a seller that gives the buyer the right--but not the obligation-- to buy or to sell a particular asset (the underlying asset) at a later day at an agreed price. In return for granting the _____, the seller collects a payment (the premium) from the buyer. A call _____ gives the buyer the right to buy the underlying asset; a put _____ gives the buyer of the _____ the right to sell the underlying asset.
   a. Option
   b. ADTECH
   c. AMAX
   d. ACNielsen

9. _____ generally refers to a list of all planned expenses and revenues. It is a plan for saving and spending. A _____ is an important concept in microeconomics, which uses a _____ line to illustrate the trade-offs between two or more goods.
   a. 180SearchAssistant
   b. Power III
   c. 6-3-5 Brainwriting
   d. Budget

10. _____ is subcontracting a process, such as product design or manufacturing, to a third-party company. The decision to outsource is often made in the interest of lowering cost or making better use of time and energy costs, redirecting or conserving energy directed at the competencies of a particular business, or to make more efficient use of land, labor, capital, (information) technology and resources. _____ became part of the business lexicon during the 1980s.
   a. Outsourcing
   b. In-house
   c. ACNielsen
   d. Intangible assets

11. _____ refer to a collection of facts usually collected as the result of experience, observation or experiment or a set of premises. This may consist of numbers, words particularly as measurements or observations of a set of variables. _____ are often viewed as a lowest level of abstraction from which information and knowledge are derived.

a. Pearson product-moment correlation coefficient
b. Data
c. Sample size
d. Mean

12. _____ refers to the structured transmission of data between organizations by electronic means. It is used to transfer electronic documents from one computer system to another (ie) from one trading partner to another trading partner. It is more than mere E-mail; for instance, organizations might replace bills of lading and even checks with appropriate _____ messages.
   a. ADTECH
   b. AMAX
   c. ACNielsen
   d. Electronic Data Interchange

13. _____ is the realization of an application idea, model, design, specification, standard, algorithm an _____ is a realization of a technical specification or algorithm as a program, software component, or other computer system. Many _____s may exist for a given specification or standard.
   a. Implementation
   b. AMAX
   c. ACNielsen
   d. ADTECH

14. In economics, business, retail, and accounting, a _____ is the value of money that has been used up to produce something, and hence is not available for use anymore. In economics, a _____ is an alternative that is given up as a result of a decision. In business, the _____ may be one of acquisition, in which case the amount of money expended to acquire it is counted as _____.
   a. Transaction cost
   b. Fixed costs
   c. Variable cost
   d. Cost

Chapter 3. STRATEGIC CRM

1. _____ consists of the processes a company uses to track and organize its contacts with its current and prospective customers. _____ software is used to support these processes; information about customers and customer interactions can be entered, stored and accessed by employees in different company departments. Typical _____ goals are to improve services provided to customers, and to use customer contact information for targeted marketing.
    a. Product bundling
    b. Customer relationship management
    c. Commercialization
    d. Demand generation

2. _____s are structured marketing efforts that reward, and therefore encourage, loyal buying behaviour -- behaviour which is potentially of benefit to the firm.

   In marketing generally and in retailing more specifically, a loyalty card, rewards card, points card, advantage card, or club card is a plastic or paper card, visually similar to a credit card or debit card, that identifies the card holder as a member in a _____. Loyalty cards are a system of the loyalty business model.

    a. Power III
    b. 180SearchAssistant
    c. Loyalty program
    d. 6-3-5 Brainwriting

3. Customer _____ consists of the processes a company uses to track and organize its contacts with its current and prospective customers. CRelationship management software is used to support these processes; information about customers and customer interactions can be entered, stored and accessed by employees in different company departments. Typical CRelationship management goals are to improve services provided to customers, and to use customer contact information for targeted marketing.
    a. Green marketing
    b. Product bundling
    c. Marketing
    d. Relationship management

4. _____ generally refers to a list of all planned expenses and revenues. It is a plan for saving and spending. A _____ is an important concept in microeconomics, which uses a _____ line to illustrate the trade-offs between two or more goods.
    a. 180SearchAssistant
    b. 6-3-5 Brainwriting
    c. Power III
    d. Budget

Chapter 3. STRATEGIC CRM

5. A _____ is a framework for creating economic, social, and/or other forms of value. The term _____ is thus used for a broad range of informal and formal descriptions to represent core aspects of a business, including purpose, offerings, strategies, infrastructure, organizational structures, trading practices, and operational processes and policies.

In the most basic sense, a _____ is the method of doing business by which a company can sustain itself -- that is, generate revenue.

   a. Service provider
   b. Pay to surf
   c. Business model
   d. Yield management

6. _____ is the realization of an application idea, model, design, specification, standard, algorithm an _____ is a realization of a technical specification or algorithm as a program, software component, or other computer system. Many _____s may exist for a given specification or standard.
   a. AMAX
   b. Implementation
   c. ACNielsen
   d. ADTECH

7. _____ refer to a collection of facts usually collected as the result of experience, observation or experiment or a set of premises. This may consist of numbers, words particularly as measurements or observations of a set of variables. _____ are often viewed as a lowest level of abstraction from which information and knowledge are derived.
   a. Sample size
   b. Pearson product-moment correlation coefficient
   c. Mean
   d. Data

8. _____ refers to the structured transmission of data between organizations by electronic means. It is used to transfer electronic documents from one computer system to another (ie) from one trading partner to another trading partner. It is more than mere E-mail; for instance, organizations might replace bills of lading and even checks with appropriate _____ messages.
   a. ADTECH
   b. Electronic Data Interchange
   c. ACNielsen
   d. AMAX

Chapter 3. STRATEGIC CRM

9. In economics, an externality or spillover of an economic transaction is an impact on a party that is not directly involved in the transaction. In such a case, prices do not reflect the full costs or benefits in production or consumption of a product or service. A positive impact is called an _____ benefit, while a negative impact is called an _____ cost.

   a. ACNielsen
   b. External
   c. ADTECH
   d. AMAX

10. _____ is defined by the American _____ Association as the activity, set of institutions, and processes for creating, communicating, delivering, and exchanging offerings that have value for customers, clients, partners, and society at large. The term developed from the original meaning which referred literally to going to market, as in shopping, or going to a market to sell goods or services.

    _____ practice tends to be seen as a creative industry, which includes advertising, distribution and selling.

    a. Product naming
    b. Marketing
    c. Customer acquisition management
    d. Marketing myopia

11. _____ is an advertisement in which a particular product specifically mentions a competitor by name for the express purpose of showing why the competitor is inferior to the product naming it.

    This should not be confused with parody advertisements, where a fictional product is being advertised for the purpose of poking fun at the particular advertisement, nor should it be confused with the use of a coined brand name for the purpose of comparing the product without actually naming an actual competitor. ('Wikipedia tastes better and is less filling than the Encyclopedia Galactica.')

    In the 1980s, during what has been referred to as the cola wars, soft-drink manufacturer Pepsi ran a series of advertisements where people, caught on hidden camera, in a blind taste test, chose Pepsi over rival Coca-Cola.

    a. Comparative advertising
    b. Heavy-up
    c. Cost per conversion
    d. GL-70

12. A _____ is a plan of action designed to achieve a particular goal.

_____ is different from tactics. In military terms, tactics is concerned with the conduct of an engagement while _____ is concerned with how different engagements are linked.

a. Power III
b. 180SearchAssistant
c. Strategy
d. 6-3-5 Brainwriting

13. A personal and cultural _____ is a relative ethic _____, an assumption upon which implementation can be extrapolated. A _____ system is a set of consistent _____s and measures that is soo not true. A principle _____ is a foundation upon which other _____s and measures of integrity are based.
a. Supreme Court of the United States
b. Perceptual maps
c. Package-on-Package
d. Value

14. In the field of marketing, a customer _____ consists of the sum total of benefits which a vendor promises that a customer will receive in return for the customer's associated payment (or other value-transfer.)

Put simply, the _____ is what the customer gets for his money.

Accordingly, a customer can evaluate a company's value-proposition on two broad dimensions with multiple subsets:

1. relative performance: what the customer gets from the vendor relative to a competitor's offering;
2. price: which consists of the payment the customer makes to acquire the product or service; plus the access cost

The vendor-company's marketing and sales efforts offer a customer _____; the vendor-company's delivery and customer-service processes then fulfill that value-proposition.

A value-proposition can assist in a firm's marketing strategy, and may guide a business to target a particular market segment.

a. Value proposition
b. Marketing performance measurement and management
c. Relationship management
d. DefCom Australia

Chapter 3. STRATEGIC CRM

15. Competitiveness is a comparative concept of the ability and performance of a firm, sub-sector or country to sell and supply goods and/or services in a given market. Although widely used in economics and business management, the usefulness of the concept, particularly in the context of national competitiveness, is vigorously disputed by economists, such as Paul Krugman .

The term may also be applied to markets, where it is used to refer to the extent to which the market structure may be regarded as perfectly _____.

   a. Geographical pricing
   b. Customs union
   c. Free trade zone
   d. Competitive

16. A supply chain is the system of organizations, people, technology, activities, information and resources involved in moving a product or service from _____ to customer. Supply chain activities transform natural resources, raw materials and components into a finished product that is delivered to the end customer. In sophisticated supply chain systems, used products may re-enter the supply chain at any point where residual value is recyclable.
   a. Supplier
   b. Rebate
   c. Bringin' Home the Oil
   d. Product line extension

17. A _____ or logistics network is the system of organizations, people, technology, activities, information and resources involved in moving a product or service from supplier to customer. _____ activities transform natural resources, raw materials and components into a finished product that is delivered to the end customer. In sophisticated _____ systems, used products may re-enter the _____ at any point where residual value is recyclable.
   a. Supply chain network
   b. Demand chain management
   c. Purchasing
   d. Supply chain

18. _____ is a contract between two parties, one being the employer and the other being the employee. An employee may be defined as: 'A person in the service of another under any contract of hire, express or implied, oral or written, where the employer has the power or right to control and direct the employee in the material details of how the work is to be performed.' Black's Law Dictionary page 471 (5th ed. 1979.)

a. ADTECH
b. ACNielsen
c. AMAX
d. Employment

19. _____ is an ongoing process that occurs strictly within a company or organization whereby the functional process aligns, motivates and empowers employees at all management levels to consistently deliver a satisfying customer experience. According to Burkitt and Zealley, 'the challenge for _____ is not only to get the right messages across, but to embed them in such a way that they both change and reinforce employee behaviour'.

a. Internal marketing
b. AMAX
c. ACNielsen
d. ADTECH

Chapter 4. IMPLEMENTING THE CRM STRATEGY

1. _____ is the realization of an application idea, model, design, specification, standard, algorithm an _____ is a realization of a technical specification or algorithm as a program, software component, or other computer system. Many _____s may exist for a given specification or standard.
   a. AMAX
   b. ACNielsen
   c. Implementation
   d. ADTECH

2. Importance of _____ is critical for any commercial organization. Expanding business is not possible without increasing sales volumes, and effective _____ goal is to organize sales team work in such a manner that ensures a growing flow of regular customers and increasing amount of sales.

The four phase-model of Management Process

1. Conception
2. Planning
3. Execution
4. Control

This model is cyclical, so it is a constant/continuous process.

===_____ is attainment of sales force goals in a effective ' efficient manner through planning, staffing, training, leading ' controlling organizational resources.

   a. Sales process
   b. Hit rate
   c. Request for proposal
   d. Sales management

3. _____ consists of the processes a company uses to track and organize its contacts with its current and prospective customers. _____ software is used to support these processes; information about customers and customer interactions can be entered, stored and accessed by employees in different company departments. Typical _____ goals are to improve services provided to customers, and to use customer contact information for targeted marketing.
   a. Product bundling
   b. Customer relationship management
   c. Commercialization
   d. Demand generation

4. _____ is the provision of service to customers before, during and after a purchase.

Chapter 4. IMPLEMENTING THE CRM STRATEGY

According to Turban et al., '_____ is a series of activities designed to enhance the level of customer satisfaction - that is, the feeling that a product or service has met the customer expectation.'

Its importance varies by product, industry and customer.

a. Facing
b. Customer service
c. COPC Inc.
d. Customer experience

5. Customer _____ consists of the processes a company uses to track and organize its contacts with its current and prospective customers. CRelationship management software is used to support these processes; information about customers and customer interactions can be entered, stored and accessed by employees in different company departments. Typical CRelationship management goals are to improve services provided to customers, and to use customer contact information for targeted marketing.

a. Marketing
b. Product bundling
c. Green marketing
d. Relationship management

6. _____ is an advertisement in which a particular product specifically mentions a competitor by name for the express purpose of showing why the competitor is inferior to the product naming it.

This should not be confused with parody advertisements, where a fictional product is being advertised for the purpose of poking fun at the particular advertisement, nor should it be confused with the use of a coined brand name for the purpose of comparing the product without actually naming an actual competitor. ('Wikipedia tastes better and is less filling than the Encyclopedia Galactica.')

In the 1980s, during what has been referred to as the cola wars, soft-drink manufacturer Pepsi ran a series of advertisements where people, caught on hidden camera, in a blind taste test, chose Pepsi over rival Coca-Cola.

a. Comparative advertising
b. GL-70
c. Cost per conversion
d. Heavy-up

Chapter 4. IMPLEMENTING THE CRM STRATEGY

7. _____ generally refers to a list of all planned expenses and revenues. It is a plan for saving and spending. A _____ is an important concept in microeconomics, which uses a _____ line to illustrate the trade-offs between two or more goods.
   a. Power III
   b. 6-3-5 Brainwriting
   c. Budget
   d. 180SearchAssistant

8. In economics, business, retail, and accounting, a _____ is the value of money that has been used up to produce something, and hence is not available for use anymore. In economics, a _____ is an alternative that is given up as a result of a decision. In business, the _____ may be one of acquisition, in which case the amount of money expended to acquire it is counted as _____.
   a. Variable cost
   b. Transaction cost
   c. Cost
   d. Fixed costs

9. _____ refer to a collection of facts usually collected as the result of experience, observation or experiment or a set of premises. This may consist of numbers, words particularly as measurements or observations of a set of variables. _____ are often viewed as a lowest level of abstraction from which information and knowledge are derived.
   a. Mean
   b. Sample size
   c. Pearson product-moment correlation coefficient
   d. Data

10. _____ is the study of when, why, how, where and what people do or do not buy products. It blends elements from psychology, sociology, social psychology, anthropology and economics. It attempts to understand the buyer decision making process, both individually and in groups. It studies characteristics of individual consumers such as demographics and behavioural variables in an attempt to understand people's wants. It also tries to assess influences on the consumer from groups such as family, friends, reference groups, and society in general.
    a. Consumer confidence
    b. Multidimensional scaling
    c. Consumer behavior
    d. Communal marketing

Chapter 4. IMPLEMENTING THE CRM STRATEGY

11. _____ or _____ data refers to selected population characteristics as used in government, marketing or opinion research, or the _____ profiles used in such research. Note the distinction from the term 'demography' Commonly-used _____ include race, age, income, disabilities, mobility (in terms of travel time to work or number of vehicles available), educational attainment, home ownership, employment status, and even location.
   a. African Americans
   b. AStore
   c. Albert Einstein
   d. Demographic

12. _____ refers to the structured transmission of data between organizations by electronic means. It is used to transfer electronic documents from one computer system to another (ie) from one trading partner to another trading partner. It is more than mere E-mail; for instance, organizations might replace bills of lading and even checks with appropriate _____ messages.
   a. ADTECH
   b. AMAX
   c. ACNielsen
   d. Electronic Data Interchange

13. _____ is the set of reasons that determines one to engage in a particular behavior. The term is generally used for human _____ but, theoretically, it can be used to describe the causes for animal behavior as well
   a. 180SearchAssistant
   b. Power III
   c. Role playing
   d. Motivation

14. A _____ is a plan of action designed to achieve a particular goal.

_____ is different from tactics. In military terms, tactics is concerned with the conduct of an engagement while _____ is concerned with how different engagements are linked.

   a. 180SearchAssistant
   b. Strategy
   c. Power III
   d. 6-3-5 Brainwriting

Chapter 4. IMPLEMENTING THE CRM STRATEGY

15. _____ is defined by the Oxford English Dictionary as 'the action or practice of selling among or between established clients, markets, traders, etc.' or 'that of selling an additional product or service to an existing customer'. In practice businesses define _____ in many different ways. Elements that might influence the definition might include: the size of the business, the industry sector it operates within and the financial motivations of those required to define the term.

   a. Freebie marketing
   b. Yield management
   c. Service provider
   d. Cross-selling

16. A _____ is a framework for creating economic, social, and/or other forms of value. The term _____ is thus used for a broad range of informal and formal descriptions to represent core aspects of a business, including purpose, offerings, strategies, infrastructure, organizational structures, trading practices, and operational processes and policies.

   In the most basic sense, a _____ is the method of doing business by which a company can sustain itself -- that is, generate revenue.

   a. Service provider
   b. Pay to surf
   c. Yield management
   d. Business model

17. _____ is defined by the American _____ Association as the activity, set of institutions, and processes for creating, communicating, delivering, and exchanging offerings that have value for customers, clients, partners, and society at large. The term developed from the original meaning which referred literally to going to market, as in shopping, or going to a market to sell goods or services.

   _____ practice tends to be seen as a creative industry, which includes advertising, distribution and selling.

   a. Marketing myopia
   b. Customer acquisition management
   c. Product naming
   d. Marketing

Chapter 4. IMPLEMENTING THE CRM STRATEGY

18. Human beings are also considered to be _____ because they have the ability to change raw materials into valuable _____. The term Human _____ can also be defined as the skills, energies, talents, abilities and knowledge that are used for the production of goods or the rendering of services. While taking into account human beings as _____, the following things have to be kept in mind:

- The size of the population
- The capabilities of the individuals in that population

Many _____ cannot be consumed in their original form. They have to be processed in order to change them into more usable commodities.

a. 180SearchAssistant
b. 6-3-5 Brainwriting
c. Power III
d. Resources

19. _____ is difficult to define. For example, in 1952, Alfred Kroeber and Clyde Kluckhohn compiled a list of 164 definitions of '_____' in _____: A Critical Review of Concepts and Definitions. However, the word '_____' is most commonly used in three basic senses:

- excellence of taste in the fine arts and humanities
- an integrated pattern of human knowledge, belief, and behavior that depends upon the capacity for symbolic thought and social learning
- the set of shared attitudes, values, goals, and practices that characterizes an institution, organization or group.

When the concept first emerged in eighteenth- and nineteenth-century Europe, it connoted a process of cultivation or improvement, as in agriculture or horticulture. In the nineteenth century, it came to refer first to the betterment or refinement of the individual, especially through education, and then to the fulfillment of national aspirations or ideals.

a. African Americans
b. Albert Einstein
c. AStore
d. Culture

20. An _____ is the manufacturing of a good or service within a category. Although _____ is a broad term for any kind of economic production, in economics and urban planning _____ is a synonym for the secondary sector, which is a type of economic activity involved in the manufacturing of raw materials into goods and products.

Chapter 4. IMPLEMENTING THE CRM STRATEGY

There are four key industrial economic sectors: the primary sector, largely raw material extraction industries such as mining and farming; the secondary sector, involving refining, construction, and manufacturing; the tertiary sector, which deals with services (such as law and medicine) and distribution of manufactured goods; and the quaternary sector, a relatively new type of knowledge _____ focusing on technological research, design and development such as computer programming, and biochemistry.

a. AMAX
b. ADTECH
c. ACNielsen
d. Industry

21. _____ is a term commonly used to describe commerce transactions between businesses like the one between a manufacturer and a wholesaler or a wholesaler and a retailer i.e both the buyer and the seller are business entity. This is unlike business-to-consumers (B2C) which involve a business entity and end consumer, or business-to-government (B2G) which involve a business entity and government.

The volume of B2B transactions is much higher than the volume of B2C transactions. The primary reason for this is that in a typical supply chain there will be many B2B transactions involving subcomponent or raw materials, and only one B2C transaction, specifically sale of the finished product to the end customer.

a. Customer relationship management
b. Social marketing
c. Business-to-business
d. Disruptive technology

Chapter 5. INTRODUCTION TO CUSTOMER-BASED MARKETING METRICS

1. _____, in strategic management and marketing, is the percentage or proportion of the total available market or market segment that is being serviced by a company. It can be expressed as a company's sales revenue (from that market) divided by the total sales revenue available in that market. It can also be expressed as a company's unit sales volume (in a market) divided by the total volume of units sold in that market.
   a. Market share
   b. Cyberdoc
   c. Customer relationship management
   d. Demand generation

2. A personal and cultural _____ is a relative ethic _____, an assumption upon which implementation can be extrapolated. A _____ system is a set of consistent _____s and measures that is soo not true. A principle _____ is a foundation upon which other _____s and measures of integrity are based.
   a. Value
   b. Supreme Court of the United States
   c. Perceptual maps
   d. Package-on-Package

3. In economics, business, retail, and accounting, a _____ is the value of money that has been used up to produce something, and hence is not available for use anymore. In economics, a _____ is an alternative that is given up as a result of a decision. In business, the _____ may be one of acquisition, in which case the amount of money expended to acquire it is counted as _____.
   a. Transaction cost
   b. Cost
   c. Variable cost
   d. Fixed costs

4. _____s are structured marketing efforts that reward, and therefore encourage, loyal buying behaviour -- behaviour which is potentially of benefit to the firm.

In marketing generally and in retailing more specifically, a loyalty card, rewards card, points card, advantage card, or club card is a plastic or paper card, visually similar to a credit card or debit card, that identifies the card holder as a member in a _____. Loyalty cards are a system of the loyalty business model.

   a. 6-3-5 Brainwriting
   b. 180SearchAssistant
   c. Loyalty program
   d. Power III

Chapter 5. INTRODUCTION TO CUSTOMER-BASED MARKETING METRICS

5. _____ is defined by the American _____ Association as the activity, set of institutions, and processes for creating, communicating, delivering, and exchanging offerings that have value for customers, clients, partners, and society at large. The term developed from the original meaning which referred literally to going to market, as in shopping, or going to a market to sell goods or services.

_____ practice tends to be seen as a creative industry, which includes advertising, distribution and selling.

   a. Marketing myopia
   b. Product naming
   c. Customer acquisition management
   d. Marketing

6. In mathematics, an _____, or central tendency of a data set refers to a measure of the 'middle' or 'expected' value of the data set. There are many different descriptive statistics that can be chosen as a measurement of the central tendency of the data items.

An _____ is a single value that is meant to typify a list of values.

   a. Average
   b. ACNielsen
   c. AMAX
   d. ADTECH

7. _____ is a way of expressing knowledge or belief that an event will occur or has occurred. In mathematics the concept has been given an exact meaning in _____ theory, that is used extensively in such areas of study as mathematics, statistics, finance, gambling, science, and philosophy to draw conclusions about the likelihood of potential events and the underlying mechanics of complex systems.
   a. Linear regression
   b. Data
   c. Heteroskedastic
   d. Probability

8. _____ is a term commonly used to describe commerce transactions between businesses like the one between a manufacturer and a wholesaler or a wholesaler and a retailer i.e both the buyer and the seller are business entity. This is unlike business-to-consumers (B2C) which involve a business entity and end consumer, or business-to-government (B2G) which involve a business entity and government.

The volume of B2B transactions is much higher than the volume of B2C transactions. The primary reason for this is that in a typical supply chain there will be many B2B transactions involving subcomponent or raw materials, and only one B2C transaction, specifically sale of the finished product to the end customer.

Chapter 5. INTRODUCTION TO CUSTOMER-BASED MARKETING METRICS

a. Customer relationship management
b. Business-to-business
c. Social marketing
d. Disruptive technology

9. _____ is the realization of an application idea, model, design, specification, standard, algorithm an _____ is a realization of a technical specification or algorithm as a program, software component, or other computer system. Many _____s may exist for a given specification or standard.

a. AMAX
b. Implementation
c. ADTECH
d. ACNielsen

10. The phrase _____ refers to the aspect of corporate strategy, corporate finance and management dealing with the buying, selling and combining of different companies that can aid, finance, or help a growing company in a given industry grow rapidly without having to create another business entity.

An acquisition, also known as a takeover or a buyout, is the buying of one company (the 'target') by another. An acquisition may be friendly or hostile.

a. Mergers and acquisitions
b. Power III
c. 6-3-5 Brainwriting
d. 180SearchAssistant

11. In marketing, customer _____, lifetime customer value (LCV), or _____ (LTV) and a new concept of 'customer life cycle management' is the present value of the future cash flows attributed to the customer relationship. Use of customer _____ as a marketing metric tends to place greater emphasis on customer service and long-term customer satisfaction, rather than on maximizing short-term sales.

Customer _____ has intuitive appeal as a marketing concept, because in theory it represents exactly how much each customer is worth in monetary terms, and therefore exactly how much a marketing department should be willing to spend to acquire each customer.

a. Value chain
b. Lifetime value
c. Brand infiltration
d. Sweepstakes

Chapter 5. INTRODUCTION TO CUSTOMER-BASED MARKETING METRICS

12. The most important feature of a contract is that one party makes an _____ for an arrangement that another accepts. This can be called a 'concurrence of wills' or 'ad idem' (meeting of the minds) of two or more parties. The concept is somewhat contested.
    a. ADTECH
    b. ACNielsen
    c. Offer
    d. AMAX

Chapter 6. CUSTOMER VALUE METRICS-CONCEPTS AND PRACTICES

1. _____ generally refers to a list of all planned expenses and revenues. It is a plan for saving and spending. A _____ is an important concept in microeconomics, which uses a _____ line to illustrate the trade-offs between two or more goods.
    a. Budget
    b. Power III
    c. 6-3-5 Brainwriting
    d. 180SearchAssistant

2. A personal and cultural _____ is a relative ethic _____, an assumption upon which implementation can be extrapolated. A _____ system is a set of consistent _____s and measures that is soo not true. A principle _____ is a foundation upon which other _____s and measures of integrity are based.
    a. Supreme Court of the United States
    b. Perceptual maps
    c. Package-on-Package
    d. Value

3.

The net present value (NPV) of all of a company's customers in terms of customer loyalty and indirectly, the revenue that the company can obtain from them.

In deciding the value of a company, it is important to know of how much value its customer base is in terms of future revenues. The greater the _____ , the more future revenue in the lifetime of its clients; this means that a company with a higher _____ can get more money from its customers on average than another company that is identical in all other characteristics.

   a. Product proliferation
   b. Marginal revenue
   c. Total cost
   d. Customer equity

4. In marketing, customer _____, lifetime customer value (LCV), or _____ (LTV) and a new concept of 'customer life cycle management' is the present value of the future cash flows attributed to the customer relationship. Use of customer _____ as a marketing metric tends to place greater emphasis on customer service and long-term customer satisfaction, rather than on maximizing short-term sales.

Customer _____ has intuitive appeal as a marketing concept, because in theory it represents exactly how much each customer is worth in monetary terms, and therefore exactly how much a marketing department should be willing to spend to acquire each customer.

Chapter 6. CUSTOMER VALUE METRICS-CONCEPTS AND PRACTICES

   a. Value chain
   b. Brand infiltration
   c. Sweepstakes
   d. Lifetime value

5. _____ is the realization of an application idea, model, design, specification, standard, algorithm an _____ is a realization of a technical specification or algorithm as a program, software component, or other computer system. Many _____s may exist for a given specification or standard.
   a. AMAX
   b. ADTECH
   c. ACNielsen
   d. Implementation

6. _____, in strategic management and marketing, is the percentage or proportion of the total available market or market segment that is being serviced by a company. It can be expressed as a company's sales revenue (from that market) divided by the total sales revenue available in that market. It can also be expressed as a company's unit sales volume (in a market) divided by the total volume of units sold in that market.
   a. Demand generation
   b. Market share
   c. Customer relationship management
   d. Cyberdoc

7. Procter is a surname, and may also refer to:

   - Bryan Waller Procter (pseud. Barry Cornwall), English poet
   - Goodwin Procter, American law firm
   - _____, consumer products multinational

   a. Black PRies
   b. Procter ' Gamble
   c. Convergent
   d. Flyer

8. _____ is a costing model that identifies activities in an organization and assigns the cost of each activity resource to all products and services according to the actual consumption by each: it assigns more indirect costs (overhead) into direct costs.

Chapter 6. CUSTOMER VALUE METRICS-CONCEPTS AND PRACTICES

In this way an organization can establish the true cost of its individual products and services for the purposes of identifying and eliminating those which are unprofitable and lowering the prices of those which are overpriced.

In a business organization, the ABC methodology assigns an organization's resource costs through activities to the products and services provided to its customers.

a. Activity-based costing
b. ACNielsen
c. AMAX
d. ADTECH

9. _____s are used in open sentences. For instance, in the formula x + 1 = 5, x is a _____ which represents an 'unknown' number. _____s are often represented by letters of the Roman alphabet, or those of other alphabets, such as Greek, and use other special symbols.
a. Personalization
b. Book of business
c. Quantitative
d. Variable

10. In statistics, _____ is a collective name for techniques for the modeling and analysis of numerical data consisting of values of a dependent variable and of one or more independent variables The dependent variable in the regression equation is modeled as a function of the independent variables, corresponding parameters, and an error term. The error term is treated as a random variable.
a. Regression analysis
b. Variance inflation factor
c. Stepwise regression
d. Multicollinearity

Chapter 7. USING DATABASES

1. _____ refers to the evolving trend in marketing whereby marketing has moved from a transaction-based effort to a conversation. The definition of _____ comes from John Deighton at Harvard, who says _____ is the ability to address the customer, remember what the customer says and address the customer again in a way that illustrates that we remember what the customer has told us (Deighton 1996.) _____ is not synonymous with online marketing, although _____ processes are facilitated by internet technology.

   a. European Information Technology Observatory
   b. Outsourcing relationship management
   c. InfoNU
   d. Interactive marketing

2. _____ is defined by the American _____ Association as the activity, set of institutions, and processes for creating, communicating, delivering, and exchanging offerings that have value for customers, clients, partners, and society at large. The term developed from the original meaning which referred literally to going to market, as in shopping, or going to a market to sell goods or services.

   _____ practice tends to be seen as a creative industry, which includes advertising, distribution and selling.

   a. Product naming
   b. Customer acquisition management
   c. Marketing
   d. Marketing myopia

3. A _____ is a structured collection of records or data that is stored in a computer system. The structure is achieved by organizing the data according to a _____ model. The model in most common use today is the relational model.

   a. Power III
   b. 180SearchAssistant
   c. Database
   d. 6-3-5 Brainwriting

4. _____ refer to a collection of facts usually collected as the result of experience, observation or experiment or a set of premises. This may consist of numbers, words particularly as measurements or observations of a set of variables. _____ are often viewed as a lowest level of abstraction from which information and knowledge are derived.

   a. Mean
   b. Pearson product-moment correlation coefficient
   c. Sample size
   d. Data

Chapter 7. USING DATABASES

5. _____ refers to the structured transmission of data between organizations by electronic means. It is used to transfer electronic documents from one computer system to another (ie) from one trading partner to another trading partner. It is more than mere E-mail; for instance, organizations might replace bills of lading and even checks with appropriate _____ messages.
   a. ACNielsen
   b. Electronic Data Interchange
   c. ADTECH
   d. AMAX

6. _____ generally refers to a list of all planned expenses and revenues. It is a plan for saving and spending. A _____ is an important concept in microeconomics, which uses a _____ line to illustrate the trade-offs between two or more goods.
   a. 180SearchAssistant
   b. Power III
   c. Budget
   d. 6-3-5 Brainwriting

Chapter 8. DESIGNING LOYALTY PROGRAMS

1. _____, a business term, is a measure of how products and services supplied by a company meet or surpass customer expectation. It is seen as a key performance indicator within business and is part of the four perspectives of a Balanced Scorecard.

In a competitive marketplace where businesses compete for customers, _____ is seen as a key differentiator and increasingly has become a key element of business strategy.

   a. Psychological pricing
   b. Customer satisfaction
   c. Supplier diversity
   d. Customer base

2. Procter is a surname, and may also refer to:

   - Bryan Waller Procter (pseud. Barry Cornwall), English poet
   - Goodwin Procter, American law firm
   - _____, consumer products multinational

   a. Convergent
   b. Procter ' Gamble
   c. Flyer
   d. Black PRies

3. _____ is an advertisement in which a particular product specifically mentions a competitor by name for the express purpose of showing why the competitor is inferior to the product naming it.

This should not be confused with parody advertisements, where a fictional product is being advertised for the purpose of poking fun at the particular advertisement, nor should it be confused with the use of a coined brand name for the purpose of comparing the product without actually naming an actual competitor. ('Wikipedia tastes better and is less filling than the Encyclopedia Galactica.')

In the 1980s, during what has been referred to as the cola wars, soft-drink manufacturer Pepsi ran a series of advertisements where people, caught on hidden camera, in a blind taste test, chose Pepsi over rival Coca-Cola.

   a. Cost per conversion
   b. Comparative advertising
   c. Heavy-up
   d. GL-70

Chapter 8. DESIGNING LOYALTY PROGRAMS 35

4. A personal and cultural _____ is a relative ethic _____, an assumption upon which implementation can be extrapolated. A _____ system is a set of consistent _____s and measures that is soo not true. A principle _____ is a foundation upon which other _____s and measures of integrity are based.
   a. Perceptual maps
   b. Value
   c. Supreme Court of the United States
   d. Package-on-Package

5. In environmental modeling and especially in hydrology, a _____ model means a model that is acceptably consistent with observed natural processes, i.e. that simulates well, for example, observed river discharge. It is a key concept of the so-called Generalized Likelihood Uncertainty Estimation (GLUE) methodology to quantify how uncertain environmental predictions are.
   a. 180SearchAssistant
   b. Power III
   c. 6-3-5 Brainwriting
   d. Behavioral

6. _____s are structured marketing efforts that reward, and therefore encourage, loyal buying behaviour -- behaviour which is potentially of benefit to the firm.

In marketing generally and in retailing more specifically, a loyalty card, rewards card, points card, advantage card, or club card is a plastic or paper card, visually similar to a credit card or debit card, that identifies the card holder as a member in a _____. Loyalty cards are a system of the loyalty business model.

   a. 180SearchAssistant
   b. 6-3-5 Brainwriting
   c. Power III
   d. Loyalty program

7. _____ refer to a collection of facts usually collected as the result of experience, observation or experiment or a set of premises. This may consist of numbers, words particularly as measurements or observations of a set of variables. _____ are often viewed as a lowest level of abstraction from which information and knowledge are derived.
   a. Sample size
   b. Pearson product-moment correlation coefficient
   c. Mean
   d. Data

Chapter 8. DESIGNING LOYALTY PROGRAMS

8. _____ is the process of extracting hidden patterns from data. As more data is gathered, with the amount of data doubling every three years, _____ is becoming an increasingly important tool to transform this data into information. It is commonly used in a wide range of profiling practices, such as marketing, surveillance, fraud detection and scientific discovery.
   a. 180SearchAssistant
   b. Data mining
   c. Structure mining
   d. Power III

9. An _____ is the manufacturing of a good or service within a category. Although _____ is a broad term for any kind of economic production, in economics and urban planning _____ is a synonym for the secondary sector, which is a type of economic activity involved in the manufacturing of raw materials into goods and products.

There are four key industrial economic sectors: the primary sector, largely raw material extraction industries such as mining and farming; the secondary sector, involving refining, construction, and manufacturing; the tertiary sector, which deals with services (such as law and medicine) and distribution of manufactured goods; and the quaternary sector, a relatively new type of knowledge _____ focusing on technological research, design and development such as computer programming, and biochemistry.

   a. ADTECH
   b. Industry
   c. ACNielsen
   d. AMAX

10. _____ generally refers to a list of all planned expenses and revenues. It is a plan for saving and spending. A _____ is an important concept in microeconomics, which uses a _____ line to illustrate the trade-offs between two or more goods.
    a. 180SearchAssistant
    b. Power III
    c. 6-3-5 Brainwriting
    d. Budget

11. _____ is the state or fact of exclusive rights and control over property, which may be an object, land/real estate, or some other kind of property (like government-granted monopolies collectively referred to as intellectual property.) It is embodied in an _____ right also referred to as title.

_____ is the key building block in the development of the capitalist socio-economic system.

a. AMAX
b. ADTECH
c. ACNielsen
d. Ownership

Chapter 9. EFFECTIVENESS OF LOYALTY PROGRAMS

1. In environmental modeling and especially in hydrology, a _____ model means a model that is acceptably consistent with observed natural processes, i.e. that simulates well, for example, observed river discharge. It is a key concept of the so-called Generalized Likelihood Uncertainty Estimation (GLUE) methodology to quantify how uncertain environmental predictions are.
    a. 6-3-5 Brainwriting
    b. 180SearchAssistant
    c. Power III
    d. Behavioral

2. _____ is a term commonly used to describe commerce transactions between businesses like the one between a manufacturer and a wholesaler or a wholesaler and a retailer i.e both the buyer and the seller are business entity.This is unlike business-to-consumers (B2C) which involve a business entity and end consumer, or business-to-government (B2G) which involve a business entity and government.

    The volume of B2B transactions is much higher than the volume of B2C transactions. The primary reason for this is that in a typical supply chain there will be many B2B transactions involving subcomponent or raw materials, and only one B2C transaction, specifically sale of the finished product to the end customer.

    a. Customer relationship management
    b. Social marketing
    c. Disruptive technology
    d. Business-to-business

3. _____ is a statistical phenomenon in marketing where, with few exceptions, brand loyalty is lower among buyers of low market share brands than buyers of high market share brands. The market leader in an industry enjoys a high level of sales due to customer loyalty, with a higher probability of repeat purchase. This phenomenon occurs because consumers believe the high sales product to be of high quality.
    a. Power III
    b. 6-3-5 Brainwriting
    c. Double jeopardy
    d. 180SearchAssistant

4. _____ is a measure of the strength of a brand, product, service relative to competitive offerings. There is often a geographic element to the competitive landscape. In defining _____, you must see to what extent a product, brand, or firm controls a product category in a given geographic area.
    a. Productivity
    b. Market system
    c. Discretionary spending
    d. Market dominance

Chapter 9. EFFECTIVENESS OF LOYALTY PROGRAMS

5. _____ is the realization of an application idea, model, design, specification, standard, algorithm an _____ is a realization of a technical specification or algorithm as a program, software component, or other computer system. Many _____s may exist for a given specification or standard.

   a. ACNielsen
   b. Implementation
   c. AMAX
   d. ADTECH

6. _____s are structured marketing efforts that reward, and therefore encourage, loyal buying behaviour -- behaviour which is potentially of benefit to the firm.

In marketing generally and in retailing more specifically, a loyalty card, rewards card, points card, advantage card, or club card is a plastic or paper card, visually similar to a credit card or debit card, that identifies the card holder as a member in a _____. Loyalty cards are a system of the loyalty business model.

   a. 6-3-5 Brainwriting
   b. 180SearchAssistant
   c. Power III
   d. Loyalty program

7. Competitiveness is a comparative concept of the ability and performance of a firm, sub-sector or country to sell and supply goods and/or services in a given market. Although widely used in economics and business management, the usefulness of the concept, particularly in the context of national competitiveness, is vigorously disputed by economists, such as Paul Krugman .

The term may also be applied to markets, where it is used to refer to the extent to which the market structure may be regarded as perfectly _____.

   a. Geographical pricing
   b. Free trade zone
   c. Customs union
   d. Competitive

8. _____ is, in very basic words, a position a firm occupies against its competitors.

According to Michael Porter, the three methods for creating a sustainable _____ are through:

1. Cost leadership - Cost advantage occurs when a firm delivers the same services as its competitors but at a lower cost;

2.

    a. 180SearchAssistant
    b. Competitive advantage
    c. Power III
    d. 6-3-5 Brainwriting

Chapter 10. DATA MINING

1. _____ refer to a collection of facts usually collected as the result of experience, observation or experiment or a set of premises. This may consist of numbers, words particularly as measurements or observations of a set of variables. _____ are often viewed as a lowest level of abstraction from which information and knowledge are derived.
    a. Pearson product-moment correlation coefficient
    b. Sample size
    c. Mean
    d. Data

2. _____ is the process of extracting hidden patterns from data. As more data is gathered, with the amount of data doubling every three years, _____ is becoming an increasingly important tool to transform this data into information. It is commonly used in a wide range of profiling practices, such as marketing, surveillance, fraud detection and scientific discovery.
    a. Power III
    b. Structure mining
    c. 180SearchAssistant
    d. Data mining

3. A personal and cultural _____ is a relative ethic _____, an assumption upon which implementation can be extrapolated. A _____ system is a set of consistent _____s and measures that is soo not true. A principle _____ is a foundation upon which other _____s and measures of integrity are based.
    a. Supreme Court of the United States
    b. Perceptual maps
    c. Package-on-Package
    d. Value

4. _____ is a term for unprocessed data, it is also known as primary data. It is a relative term _____ can be input to a computer program or used in manual analysis procedures such as gathering statistics from a survey.
    a. Product manager
    b. Shoppers Food ' Pharmacy
    c. Chief marketing officer
    d. Raw data

5. A _____ is a statement or claim that a particular event will occur in the future in more certain terms than a forecast. The etymology of this word is Latin . In regards to predicting the future Howard H. Stevenson Says, ' _____ is at least two things: Important and hard.' Important, because we have to act, and hard because we have to realize the future we want, and what is the best way to get there.

a. 6-3-5 Brainwriting
b. Prediction
c. 180SearchAssistant
d. Power III

6. _____s are used in open sentences. For instance, in the formula x + 1 = 5, x is a _____ which represents an 'unknown' number. _____s are often represented by letters of the Roman alphabet, or those of other alphabets, such as Greek, and use other special symbols.
a. Quantitative
b. Book of business
c. Personalization
d. Variable

7. _____ are used to describe the basic features of the data gathered from an experimental study in various ways. A _____ is distinguished from inductive statistics. They provide simple summaries about the sample and the measures.
a. Descriptive statistics
b. Frequency distribution
c. Pearson product-moment correlation coefficient
d. P-Value

8. _____ is a mathematical science pertaining to the collection, analysis, interpretation or explanation, and presentation of data. It also provides tools for prediction and forecasting based on data. It is applicable to a wide variety of academic disciplines, from the natural and social sciences to the humanities, government and business.
a. Median
b. Statistics
c. Type I error
d. Null hypothesis

9. _____ is the collection, deployment and translation of information that allows a business to acquire, develop and retain their customers.

Firslty, the collected data must be audited to fully understand the quality and opportunity within the database. Once this is done, there are a number of different types of analysis that can be applied.

a. Fifth screen
b. Customer insight
c. Societal marketing
d. Customer analytics

Chapter 11. CAMPAIGN MANAGEMENT

1. _____ is defined by the American _____ Association as the activity, set of institutions, and processes for creating, communicating, delivering, and exchanging offerings that have value for customers, clients, partners, and society at large. The term developed from the original meaning which referred literally to going to market, as in shopping, or going to a market to sell goods or services.

_____ practice tends to be seen as a creative industry, which includes advertising, distribution and selling.

   a. Product naming
   b. Marketing myopia
   c. Customer acquisition management
   d. Marketing

2. _____ generally refers to a list of all planned expenses and revenues. It is a plan for saving and spending. A _____ is an important concept in microeconomics, which uses a _____ line to illustrate the trade-offs between two or more goods.
   a. 6-3-5 Brainwriting
   b. 180SearchAssistant
   c. Power III
   d. Budget

3. _____ in organizations and public policy is both the organizational process of creating and maintaining a plan; and the psychological process of thinking about the activities required to create a desired goal on some scale. As such, it is a fundamental property of intelligent behavior. This thought process is essential to the creation and refinement of a plan, or integration of it with other plans, that is, it combines forecasting of developments with the preparation of scenarios of how to react to them.
   a. Power III
   b. 180SearchAssistant
   c. Planning
   d. 6-3-5 Brainwriting

4. A _____ is a plan of action designed to achieve a particular goal.

_____ is different from tactics. In military terms, tactics is concerned with the conduct of an engagement while _____ is concerned with how different engagements are linked.

   a. Power III
   b. Strategy
   c. 180SearchAssistant
   d. 6-3-5 Brainwriting

Chapter 11. CAMPAIGN MANAGEMENT

5. _____ is a term commonly used to describe commerce transactions between businesses like the one between a manufacturer and a wholesaler or a wholesaler and a retailer i.e both the buyer and the seller are business entity.This is unlike business-to-consumers (B2C) which involve a business entity and end consumer, or business-to-government (B2G) which involve a business entity and government.

The volume of B2B transactions is much higher than the volume of B2C transactions. The primary reason for this is that in a typical supply chain there will be many B2B transactions involving subcomponent or raw materials, and only one B2C transaction, specifically sale of the finished product to the end customer.

a. Customer relationship management
b. Disruptive technology
c. Social marketing
d. Business-to-business

6. _____ is the realization of an application idea, model, design, specification, standard, algorithm an _____ is a realization of a technical specification or algorithm as a program, software component, or other computer system. Many _____s may exist for a given specification or standard.
a. ADTECH
b. AMAX
c. ACNielsen
d. Implementation

7. _____ , according to The American Marketing Association, is 'a planning process designed to assure that all brand contacts received by a customer or prospect for a product, service, or organization are relevant to that person and consistent over time.' (Marketing Power Dictionary)

_____ is a term used to describe a holistic approach to marketing. It aims to ensure consistency of message and the complementary use of media. The concept includes online and offline marketing channels.

a. AMAX
b. Integrated marketing communications
c. ADTECH
d. ACNielsen

8. _____ refers to messages and related media used to communicate with a market. Those who practice advertising, branding, direct marketing, graphic design, marketing, packaging, promotion, publicity, public relations, sales, sales promotion and online marketing are termed marketing communicators, _____ managers, or more briefly as marcom managers.

a. Merchandise
b. Merchandising
c. Marketing communication
d. Sales promotion

9. The most important feature of a contract is that one party makes an _____ for an arrangement that another accepts. This can be called a 'concurrence of wills' or 'ad idem' (meeting of the minds) of two or more parties. The concept is somewhat contested.
  a. ACNielsen
  b. Offer
  c. AMAX
  d. ADTECH

10. Advertising mail junk mail is the delivery of advertising material to recipients of postal mail. The delivery of advertising mail forms a large and growing service for many postal services, and _____ marketing forms a significant portion of the direct marketing industry. Some organizations attempt to help people opt-out of receiving advertising mail, in many cases motivated by a concern over its negative environmental impact.
  a. Direct mail
  b. Phishing
  c. Directory Harvest Attack
  d. Telemarketing

11. _____s are structured marketing efforts that reward, and therefore encourage, loyal buying behaviour -- behaviour which is potentially of benefit to the firm.

In marketing generally and in retailing more specifically, a loyalty card, rewards card, points card, advantage card, or club card is a plastic or paper card, visually similar to a credit card or debit card, that identifies the card holder as a member in a _____. Loyalty cards are a system of the loyalty business model.

  a. Loyalty program
  b. 180SearchAssistant
  c. Power III
  d. 6-3-5 Brainwriting

12. _____ is a method of direct marketing in which a salesperson solicits to prospective customers to buy products or services, either over the phone or through a subsequent face to face or Web conferencing appointment scheduled during the call.

Chapter 11. CAMPAIGN MANAGEMENT

_____ can also include recorded sales pitches programmed to be played over the phone via automatic dialing. _____ has come under fire in recent years, being viewed as an annoyance by many.

a. Directory Harvest Attack
b. Telemarketing
c. Joe job
d. Phishing

13. _____ is a sales technique in which a salesperson walks from one door of a house to another trying to sell a product or service to the general public. A variant of this involves cold calling first, when another sales representative attempts to gain agreement that a salesperson should visit. _____ selling is usually conducted in the afternoon hours, when the majority of people are at home.
a. Fast moving consumer goods
b. Performance-based advertising
c. Marketing management
d. Door-to-door

14. Competitiveness is a comparative concept of the ability and performance of a firm, sub-sector or country to sell and supply goods and/or services in a given market. Although widely used in economics and business management, the usefulness of the concept, particularly in the context of national competitiveness, is vigorously disputed by economists, such as Paul Krugman .

The term may also be applied to markets, where it is used to refer to the extent to which the market structure may be regarded as perfectly _____.

a. Geographical pricing
b. Competitive
c. Customs union
d. Free trade zone

15. In economics, business, retail, and accounting, a _____ is the value of money that has been used up to produce something, and hence is not available for use anymore. In economics, a _____ is an alternative that is given up as a result of a decision. In business, the _____ may be one of acquisition, in which case the amount of money expended to acquire it is counted as _____.

Chapter 11. CAMPAIGN MANAGEMENT

a. Fixed costs
b. Cost
c. Variable cost
d. Transaction cost

16. _____ refer to a collection of facts usually collected as the result of experience, observation or experiment or a set of premises. This may consist of numbers, words particularly as measurements or observations of a set of variables. _____ are often viewed as a lowest level of abstraction from which information and knowledge are derived.

a. Data
b. Sample size
c. Pearson product-moment correlation coefficient
d. Mean

17. _____ refers to the structured transmission of data between organizations by electronic means. It is used to transfer electronic documents from one computer system to another (ie) from one trading partner to another trading partner. It is more than mere E-mail; for instance, organizations might replace bills of lading and even checks with appropriate _____ messages.

a. ADTECH
b. AMAX
c. Electronic Data Interchange
d. ACNielsen

18. In marketing, customer _____, lifetime customer value (LCV), or _____ (LTV) and a new concept of 'customer life cycle management' is the present value of the future cash flows attributed to the customer relationship. Use of customer _____ as a marketing metric tends to place greater emphasis on customer service and long-term customer satisfaction, rather than on maximizing short-term sales.

Customer _____ has intuitive appeal as a marketing concept, because in theory it represents exactly how much each customer is worth in monetary terms, and therefore exactly how much a marketing department should be willing to spend to acquire each customer.

a. Brand infiltration
b. Sweepstakes
c. Value chain
d. Lifetime value

Chapter 11. CAMPAIGN MANAGEMENT

19. A personal and cultural _____ is a relative ethic _____, an assumption upon which implementation can be extrapolated. A _____ system is a set of consistent _____s and measures that is soo not true. A principle _____ is a foundation upon which other _____s and measures of integrity are based.
   a. Supreme Court of the United States
   b. Value
   c. Perceptual maps
   d. Package-on-Package

20. Procter is a surname, and may also refer to:

   - Bryan Waller Procter (pseud. Barry Cornwall), English poet
   - Goodwin Procter, American law firm
   - _____, consumer products multinational

   a. Procter ' Gamble
   b. Convergent
   c. Black PRies
   d. Flyer

21. _____ involves disseminating information about a product, product line, brand, or company. It is one of the four key aspects of the marketing mix. (The other three elements are product marketing, pricing, and distribution). P>_____ is generally sub-divided into two parts:

   - Above the line _____: Promotion in the media (e.g. TV, radio, newspapers, Internet and Mobile Phones) in which the advertiser pays an advertising agency to place the ad
   - Below the line _____: All other _____. Much of this is intended to be subtle enough for the consumer to be unaware that _____ is taking place. E.g. sponsorship, product placement, endorsements, sales _____, merchandising, direct mail, personal selling, public relations, trade shows

   a. Davie Brown Index
   b. Cashmere Agency
   c. Promotion
   d. Bottling lines

22. _____ describes the situation when output from (or information about the result of) an event or phenomenon in the past will influence the same event/phenomenon in the present or future. When an event is part of a chain of cause-and-effect that forms a circuit or loop, then the event is said to 'feed back' into itself.

_____ is also a synonym for:

- _____ Signal; the information about the initial event that is the basis for subsequent modification of the event.
- _____ Loop; the causal path that leads from the initial generation of the _____ signal to the subsequent modification of the event.

_____ is a mechanism, process or signal that is looped back to control a system within itself. Such a loop is called a _____ loop.

a. Power III
b. Feedback
c. 180SearchAssistant
d. 6-3-5 Brainwriting

23. In statistics, an _____ is a term in a statistical model added when the effect of two or more variables is not simply additive. Such a term reflects that the effect of one variable depends on the values of one or more other variables.

Thus, for a response Y and two variables x_1 and x_2 an additive model would be:

$$Y = ax_1 + bx_2 + \text{error}$$

In contrast to this,

$$Y = ax_1 + bx_2 + c(x_1 \times x_2) + \text{error},$$

is an example of a model with an _____ between variables x_1 and x_2 ('error' refers to the random variable whose value by which y differs from the expected value of y.)

a. Interaction
b. AMAX
c. ADTECH
d. ACNielsen

Chapter 12. APPLICATIONS OF DATABASE MARKETING IN B-TO-C AND B-TO-B SCENARIOS

1. A personal and cultural _____ is a relative ethic _____, an assumption upon which implementation can be extrapolated. A _____ system is a set of consistent _____s and measures that is soo not true. A principle _____ is a foundation upon which other _____s and measures of integrity are based.
   a. Package-on-Package
   b. Supreme Court of the United States
   c. Perceptual maps
   d. Value

2. _____ is the difference between the revenues earned from and the costs associated with the customer relationship in a specified period.

According to Philip Kotler,'a profitable customer is a person, household or a company that overtime, yields a revenue stream that exceeds by an acceptable amount the company's cost stream of attracting, selling and servicing the customer'

Although _____ is nothing more than the result of applying the business concept of profit to a customer relationship, measuring the profitability of a firm's customers or customer groups can often deliver useful business insights.

Quite often a very small percentage of the firm's best customers will account for a large portion of firm profit.

   a. 180SearchAssistant
   b. Customer profitability
   c. Cost management
   d. Power III

3. _____ is a term commonly used to describe commerce transactions between businesses like the one between a manufacturer and a wholesaler or a wholesaler and a retailer i.e both the buyer and the seller are business entity.This is unlike business-to-consumers (B2C) which involve a business entity and end consumer, or business-to-government (B2G) which involve a business entity and government.

The volume of B2B transactions is much higher than the volume of B2C transactions. The primary reason for this is that in a typical supply chain there will be many B2B transactions involving subcomponent or raw materials, and only one B2C transaction, specifically sale of the finished product to the end customer.

   a. Business-to-business
   b. Social marketing
   c. Customer relationship management
   d. Disruptive technology

Chapter 12. APPLICATIONS OF DATABASE MARKETING IN B-TO-C AND B-TO-B SCENARIOS

4. _____ is a sub-discipline and type of marketing. There are two main definitional characteristics which distinguish it from other types of marketing. The first is that it attempts to send its messages directly to consumers, without the use of intervening media.
   a. Direct Marketing Associations
   b. Direct marketing
   c. Power III
   d. Database marketing

5. _____ is the realization of an application idea, model, design, specification, standard, algorithm an _____ is a realization of a technical specification or algorithm as a program, software component, or other computer system. Many _____s may exist for a given specification or standard.
   a. ADTECH
   b. Implementation
   c. AMAX
   d. ACNielsen

6. _____ is defined by the American _____ Association as the activity, set of institutions, and processes for creating, communicating, delivering, and exchanging offerings that have value for customers, clients, partners, and society at large. The term developed from the original meaning which referred literally to going to market, as in shopping, or going to a market to sell goods or services.

   _____ practice tends to be seen as a creative industry, which includes advertising, distribution and selling.

   a. Customer acquisition management
   b. Marketing myopia
   c. Product naming
   d. Marketing

7. _____ is one of the four elements of marketing mix. An organization or set of organizations (go-betweens) involved in the process of making a product or service available for use or consumption by a consumer or business user.

   The other three parts of the marketing mix are product, pricing, and promotion.

   a. Distribution
   b. Japan Advertising Photographers' Association
   c. Better Living Through Chemistry
   d. Comparison-Shopping agent

Chapter 13. APPLICATION OF THE CUSTOMER VALUE FRAMEWORK TO MARKETING DECISIONS

1. _____ is defined by the American _____ Association as the activity, set of institutions, and processes for creating, communicating, delivering, and exchanging offerings that have value for customers, clients, partners, and society at large. The term developed from the original meaning which referred literally to going to market, as in shopping, or going to a market to sell goods or services.

_____ practice tends to be seen as a creative industry, which includes advertising, distribution and selling.

a. Product naming
b. Marketing
c. Customer acquisition management
d. Marketing myopia

2. A personal and cultural _____ is a relative ethic _____, an assumption upon which implementation can be extrapolated. A _____ system is a set of consistent _____s and measures that is soo not true. A principle _____ is a foundation upon which other _____s and measures of integrity are based.
a. Perceptual maps
b. Supreme Court of the United States
c. Value
d. Package-on-Package

3. _____ generally refers to a list of all planned expenses and revenues. It is a plan for saving and spending. A _____ is an important concept in microeconomics, which uses a _____ line to illustrate the trade-offs between two or more goods.
a. Power III
b. 6-3-5 Brainwriting
c. Budget
d. 180SearchAssistant

4.

The net present value (NPV) of all of a company's customers in terms of customer loyalty and indirectly, the revenue that the company can obtain from them.

In deciding the value of a company, it is important to know of how much value its customer base is in terms of future revenues. The greater the _____ , the more future revenue in the lifetime of its clients; this means that a company with a higher _____ can get more money from its customers on average than another company that is identical in all other characteristics.

Chapter 13. APPLICATION OF THE CUSTOMER VALUE FRAMEWORK TO MARKETING DECISIONS

a. Marginal revenue
b. Customer equity
c. Product proliferation
d. Total cost

5. _____ refer to a collection of facts usually collected as the result of experience, observation or experiment or a set of premises. This may consist of numbers, words particularly as measurements or observations of a set of variables. _____ are often viewed as a lowest level of abstraction from which information and knowledge are derived.

a. Pearson product-moment correlation coefficient
b. Mean
c. Sample size
d. Data

6. _____ is the difference between the revenues earned from and the costs associated with the customer relationship in a specified period.

According to Philip Kotler,'a profitable customer is a person, household or a company that overtime, yields a revenue stream that exceeds by an acceptable amount the company's cost stream of attracting, selling and servicing the customer'

Although _____ is nothing more than the result of applying the business concept of profit to a customer relationship, measuring the profitability of a firm's customers or customer groups can often deliver useful business insights.

Quite often a very small percentage of the firm's best customers will account for a large portion of firm profit.

a. 180SearchAssistant
b. Power III
c. Cost management
d. Customer profitability

Chapter 13. APPLICATION OF THE CUSTOMER VALUE FRAMEWORK TO MARKETING DECISIONS

7. Human beings are also considered to be _____ because they have the ability to change raw materials into valuable _____. The term Human _____ can also be defined as the skills, energies, talents, abilities and knowledge that are used for the production of goods or the rendering of services. While taking into account human beings as _____, the following things have to be kept in mind:

- The size of the population
- The capabilities of the individuals in that population

Many _____ cannot be consumed in their original form. They have to be processed in order to change them into more usable commodities.

a. 6-3-5 Brainwriting
b. 180SearchAssistant
c. Power III
d. Resources

Chapter 14. IMPACT OF CRM ON MARKETING CHANNELS

1. _____ is a term commonly used to describe commerce transactions between businesses like the one between a manufacturer and a wholesaler or a wholesaler and a retailer i.e both the buyer and the seller are business entity.This is unlike business-to-consumers (B2C) which involve a business entity and end consumer, or business-to-government (B2G) which involve a business entity and government.

The volume of B2B transactions is much higher than the volume of B2C transactions. The primary reason for this is that in a typical supply chain there will be many B2B transactions involving subcomponent or raw materials, and only one B2C transaction, specifically sale of the finished product to the end customer.

   a. Business-to-business
   b. Customer relationship management
   c. Social marketing
   d. Disruptive technology

2. _____ is one of the four elements of marketing mix. An organization or set of organizations (go-betweens) involved in the process of making a product or service available for use or consumption by a consumer or business user.

The other three parts of the marketing mix are product, pricing, and promotion.

   a. Comparison-Shopping agent
   b. Distribution
   c. Japan Advertising Photographers' Association
   d. Better Living Through Chemistry

3. _____ is the realization of an application idea, model, design, specification, standard, algorithm an _____ is a realization of a technical specification or algorithm as a program, software component, or other computer system. Many _____s may exist for a given specification or standard.
   a. AMAX
   b. Implementation
   c. ACNielsen
   d. ADTECH

4. _____ is defined by the American _____ Association as the activity, set of institutions, and processes for creating, communicating, delivering, and exchanging offerings that have value for customers, clients, partners, and society at large. The term developed from the original meaning which referred literally to going to market, as in shopping, or going to a market to sell goods or services.

_____ practice tends to be seen as a creative industry, which includes advertising, distribution and selling.

Chapter 14. IMPACT OF CRM ON MARKETING CHANNELS

a. Marketing myopia
b. Customer acquisition management
c. Marketing
d. Product naming

5. _____ is marketing using many different marketing channels to reach a customer. In this sense, a channel might be a retail store, a web site, a mail order catalogue, or direct personal communications by letter, email or text message. The objective of the company doing the marketing is to make it easy for a consumer to buy from them in whatever way is most appropriate.
   a. Buy one, get one free
   b. Macromarketing
   c. Blitz QFD
   d. Multichannel marketing

6. Procter is a surname, and may also refer to:

   - Bryan Waller Procter (pseud. Barry Cornwall), English poet
   - Goodwin Procter, American law firm
   - _____, consumer products multinational

   a. Flyer
   b. Black PRies
   c. Convergent
   d. Procter ' Gamble

7. In economics and sociology, an _____ is any factor (financial or non-financial) that enables or motivates a particular course of action, or counts as a reason for preferring one choice to the alternatives. It is an expectation that encourages people to behave in a certain way. Since human beings are purposeful creatures, the study of _____ structures is central to the study of all economic activity (both in terms of individual decision-making and in terms of co-operation and competition within a larger institutional structure.)
   a. AMAX
   b. ADTECH
   c. ACNielsen
   d. Incentive

58 Chapter 14. IMPACT OF CRM ON MARKETING CHANNELS

8. _____ refer to a collection of facts usually collected as the result of experience, observation or experiment or a set of premises. This may consist of numbers, words particularly as measurements or observations of a set of variables. _____ are often viewed as a lowest level of abstraction from which information and knowledge are derived.
   a. Pearson product-moment correlation coefficient
   b. Mean
   c. Data
   d. Sample size

9. _____ refers to the structured transmission of data between organizations by electronic means. It is used to transfer electronic documents from one computer system to another (ie) from one trading partner to another trading partner. It is more than mere E-mail; for instance, organizations might replace bills of lading and even checks with appropriate _____ messages.
   a. Electronic Data Interchange
   b. AMAX
   c. ACNielsen
   d. ADTECH

10. _____,, is a common tool in the retail industry to create the look of a perfectly stocked store by pulling all of the products on a display or shelf to the front, as well as downstacking all the canned and stacked items. It is also done to keep the store appearing neat and organized.

The workers who face commonly have jobs doing other things in the store such as customer service, stocking shelves, daytime cleaning, bagging and carryouts, etc.

   a. Foviance
   b. Customer Experience Analytics
   c. Customer Integrated System
   d. Facing

11. _____ is a fee paid on borrowed assets. It is the price paid for the use of borrowed money , or, money earned by deposited funds . Assets that are sometimes lent with _____ include money, shares, consumer goods through hire purchase, major assets such as aircraft, and even entire factories in finance lease arrangements.
   a. ACNielsen
   b. ADTECH
   c. AMAX
   d. Interest

Chapter 14. IMPACT OF CRM ON MARKETING CHANNELS

12. In calculus, a function f defined on a subset of the real numbers with real values is called _____, if for all x and y such that x ≤ y one has f(x) ≤ f(y), so f preserves the order. In layman's terms, the sign of the slope is always positive (the curve tending upwards) or zero (i.e., non-decreasing, or asymptotic, or depicted as a horizontal, flat line) Likewise, a function is called monotonically decreasing (non-increasing) if, whenever x ≤ y, then f(x) ≥ f(y), so it reverses the order.
    a. Monotonic
    b. 180SearchAssistant
    c. 6-3-5 Brainwriting
    d. Power III

13. _____ is a measure of the strength of a brand, product, service relative to competitive offerings. There is often a geographic element to the competitive landscape. In defining _____, you must see to what extent a product, brand, or firm controls a product category in a given geographic area.
    a. Market dominance
    b. Productivity
    c. Discretionary spending
    d. Market system

14. _____ in organizations and public policy is both the organizational process of creating and maintaining a plan; and the psychological process of thinking about the activities required to create a desired goal on some scale. As such, it is a fundamental property of intelligent behavior. This thought process is essential to the creation and refinement of a plan, or integration of it with other plans, that is, it combines forecasting of developments with the preparation of scenarios of how to react to them.
    a. 180SearchAssistant
    b. Planning
    c. Power III
    d. 6-3-5 Brainwriting

15. _____ is an advertisement in which a particular product specifically mentions a competitor by name for the express purpose of showing why the competitor is inferior to the product naming it.

This should not be confused with parody advertisements, where a fictional product is being advertised for the purpose of poking fun at the particular advertisement, nor should it be confused with the use of a coined brand name for the purpose of comparing the product without actually naming an actual competitor. ('Wikipedia tastes better and is less filling than the Encyclopedia Galactica.')

In the 1980s, during what has been referred to as the cola wars, soft-drink manufacturer Pepsi ran a series of advertisements where people, caught on hidden camera, in a blind taste test, chose Pepsi over rival Coca-Cola.

a. Heavy-up
b. GL-70
c. Cost per conversion
d. Comparative advertising

16. _____ measures the performance of a system. Certain goals are defined and the _____ gives the percentage to which they should be achieved.

Examples

- Percentage of calls answered in a call center.
- Percentage of customers waiting less than a given fixed time.
- Percentage of customers that do not experience a stock out.

_____ is used in supply chain management and in inventory management to measure the performance of inventory systems.

Under stochastic conditions it is unavoidable that in some periods the inventory on hand is not sufficient to deliver the complete demand and, as a consequence, that part of the demand is filled only after an inventory-related waiting time.

a. Symbol group
b. Nielsen SoundScan
c. False designation of origin
d. Service level

17. In statistics, an _____ is a term in a statistical model added when the effect of two or more variables is not simply additive. Such a term reflects that the effect of one variable depends on the values of one or more other variables.

Thus, for a response Y and two variables x_1 and x_2 an additive model would be:

$$Y = ax_1 + bx_2 + \text{error}$$

In contrast to this,

$$Y = ax_1 + bx_2 + c(x_1 \times x_2) + \text{error},$$

is an example of a model with an _____ between variables x_1 and x_2 ('error' refers to the random variable whose value by which y differs from the expected value of y.)

Chapter 14. IMPACT OF CRM ON MARKETING CHANNELS

a. Interaction
b. ACNielsen
c. AMAX
d. ADTECH

18. _____s are structured marketing efforts that reward, and therefore encourage, loyal buying behaviour -- behaviour which is potentially of benefit to the firm.

In marketing generally and in retailing more specifically, a loyalty card, rewards card, points card, advantage card, or club card is a plastic or paper card, visually similar to a credit card or debit card, that identifies the card holder as a member in a _____. Loyalty cards are a system of the loyalty business model.

a. Loyalty program
b. 6-3-5 Brainwriting
c. 180SearchAssistant
d. Power III

19. A supply chain is the system of organizations, people, technology, activities, information and resources involved in moving a product or service from _____ to customer. Supply chain activities transform natural resources, raw materials and components into a finished product that is delivered to the end customer. In sophisticated supply chain systems, used products may re-enter the supply chain at any point where residual value is recyclable.
a. Bringin' Home the Oil
b. Product line extension
c. Rebate
d. Supplier

20. In environmental modeling and especially in hydrology, a _____ model means a model that is acceptably consistent with observed natural processes, i.e. that simulates well, for example, observed river discharge. It is a key concept of the so-called Generalized Likelihood Uncertainty Estimation (GLUE) methodology to quantify how uncertain environmental predictions are.
a. 180SearchAssistant
b. 6-3-5 Brainwriting
c. Behavioral
d. Power III

21. _____ is a sub-discipline and type of marketing. There are two main definitional characteristics which distinguish it from other types of marketing. The first is that it attempts to send its messages directly to consumers, without the use of intervening media.

a. Database marketing
b. Power III
c. Direct marketing
d. Direct Marketing Associations

ANSWER KEY

Chapter 1
1. a   2. d   3. d   4. a   5. b   6. b   7. b   8. d   9. d   10. d
11. c   12. d   13. b   14. d   15. d   16. d   17. d   18. b   19. d   20. d
21. d   22. b

Chapter 2
1. c   2. d   3. b   4. d   5. a   6. b   7. c   8. a   9. d   10. a
11. b   12. d   13. a   14. d

Chapter 3
1. b   2. c   3. d   4. d   5. c   6. b   7. d   8. b   9. b   10. b
11. a   12. c   13. d   14. a   15. d   16. a   17. d   18. d   19. a

Chapter 4
1. c   2. d   3. b   4. b   5. d   6. a   7. c   8. c   9. d   10. c
11. d   12. d   13. d   14. b   15. d   16. d   17. d   18. d   19. d   20. d
21. c

Chapter 5
1. a   2. a   3. b   4. c   5. d   6. a   7. d   8. b   9. b   10. a
11. b   12. c

Chapter 6
1. a   2. d   3. d   4. d   5. d   6. b   7. b   8. a   9. d   10. a

Chapter 7
1. d   2. c   3. c   4. d   5. b   6. c

Chapter 8
1. b   2. b   3. b   4. b   5. d   6. d   7. d   8. b   9. b   10. d
11. d

Chapter 9
1. d   2. d   3. c   4. d   5. b   6. d   7. d   8. b

Chapter 10
1. d   2. d   3. d   4. d   5. b   6. d   7. a   8. b   9. b

Chapter 11
1. d   2. d   3. c   4. b   5. d   6. d   7. b   8. c   9. b   10. a
11. a   12. b   13. d   14. b   15. b   16. a   17. c   18. d   19. b   20. a
21. c   22. b   23. a

Chapter 12
1. d   2. b   3. a   4. b   5. b   6. d   7. a

Chapter 13
1. b   2. c   3. c   4. b   5. d   6. d   7. d

Chapter 14
1. a   2. b   3. b   4. c   5. d   6. d   7. d   8. c   9. a   10. d
11. d   12. a   13. a   14. b   15. d   16. d   17. a   18. a   19. d   20. c
21. c

www.ingramcontent.com/pod-product-compliance
Lightning Source LLC
Chambersburg PA
CBHW080743250426
43671CB00038B/2847